D0131124

gelato

sorbet and ice cream

gelato
sorbet and ice cream

elsa petersen-schepelern
photography by
james merrell

RYLAND
PETERS
& SMALL

Art Director **Jacqui Small**

Art Editor **Penny Stock**

Editor **Elsa Petersen-Schepelern**

Photography **James Merrell**

Food Stylist **Bridget Sargeson**

Stylist **Ben Kendrick**

Production **Kate Mackillop**

Note: Some of the recipes in this book contain raw egg whites, which have been added to lighten the mixture. If you wish, omit them. In addition, uncooked eggs should not be served to the elderly, the very young, to pregnant women or to anyone with a compromised immune system. In all these recipes, the egg white may be omitted if preferred.

My thanks to Nowelle Valentina-Capezza, Sonia Stevenson, Clare Ferguson, Norah Meany, Stella Shamwana, and Tom and Jenny Merrell

First published in 1997
by Ryland Peters & Small, Inc.,
519 Broadway, 5th Floor, New York NY 10012

3 4 5 6 7 8 9 10

Printed and bound in China.

ISBN 1 84172 077 1

gelato
sorbet and ice cream

Gelato, sorbet, and ice cream can be easily made at home, thanks to the wide range of ice-cream making machines now available. But, even without a machine, you can still make these delicious recipes. Just pour the mixture into flat freezer trays, allow it to part-freeze, then beat to break up the ice crystals, and return to the freezer. Repeat several times—the more often you do it, the smoother the end result.

For gelato, it is safer to make the custard base in a double boiler, or in a bowl set over simmering water to ensure it doesn't boil or curdle. However, I always make it in a pan over a very low gas flame, and have never had a problem with curdling.

Shown right are the four main styles of ices in this book; Italian gelato, alcohol-flavored gelato, sorbet, and ice cream.

The recipes are inspired by flavors from around the world, including Italy, France, Scandinavia, India, and Southeast Asia.

gelato di crèma

A great basic Italian gelato recipe, made with cream rather than milk. It produces rather a large quantity, so divide the mixture into two or three parts, add a different flavoring to each, then churn each one separately.

4 cups heavy cream

5 egg yolks

1 cup sugar

Pour the cream into a saucepan and heat gently. Beat the egg yolks and sugar together until pale and creamy.

Beat 2 tablespoons of the hot cream into the egg mixture, then beat in the remaining cream, little by little.

Pour into a double boiler, or into a bowl set over a pan of simmering water, and cook over a gentle heat, stirring constantly, until the mixture coats the back of a spoon.

Cool, add your preferred flavorings, then churn, and serve or freeze.

Makes about 6 cups

italian gelato

traditional italian gelato

Traditional Italian gelato is made with milk rather than cream, making it denser than French ice-cream. However Italians, like all of us, love a good bout of self-indulgence, and make gelato with cream too, as you will see in the other two recipes in this chapter.

Use any of the recipes in this chapter as a basis for the different and delicious flavors you find in a Florentine *gelateria*. This one uses vanilla—and the minute black seeds in the vanilla bean give the best and most authentic taste and appearance. (Omit the vanilla if adding other flavors.)

2 vanilla beans or ½ teaspoon vanilla extract
2 cups whole milk
4 egg yolks
½ cup sugar

If using vanilla beans, split in half lengthwise. Place the beans or extract in a pan with the milk, and heat to just below boiling point. Scrape the seeds into the milk, and leave to infuse for at least 10 minutes. Stir well, then remove the beans. Reheat gently.

In a clean bowl, beat the egg yolks until creamy, then beat in 1 to 2 tablespoons of the hot milk. Beat in the remaining milk, then return the egg mixture to the saucepan, beating all the time. Stir in the sugar, then transfer to a double boiler or heatproof bowl set over a pan of simmering water. Cook over a gentle heat, stirring constantly, until the mixture coats the back of a wooden spoon. Do not allow the mixture to boil, or it will curdle. Be patient, and keep stirring.

Remove from the heat, cool, chill, then churn in an ice-cream machine according to the manufacturer's instructions, or make by hand, using freezer trays (see page 6).

Makes about 3½ cups

a **simple** gelato recipe—use it as
a base for other flavors

rich traditional gelato

2 cups milk
2 vanilla beans (see page 10), or
¼ teaspoon vanilla extract (optional)
3–4 egg yolks
½ cup sugar
1 cup heavy cream

Italian gelato is usually made with milk, as on page 10, and so is denser than French ices. Made with cream only, as on page 8, or a mixture of cream and milk, as here, it tastes even more delicious.

Both nations produce great ice-cream—though the Italians are generally thought to have the edge!

Omit the vanilla if using this recipe as a basis for other flavors.

Heat the milk with the vanilla, if using, until just below boiling point. Set aside to infuse for 15 minutes. Remove the beans. Beat the egg yolks until creamy. Beat 2 tablespoons of the hot milk into the egg mixture, then beat in the remaining milk, a little at a time.

Stir in the sugar, then transfer to a double boiler and cook over a gentle heat, stirring constantly, until the mixture coats the back of a wooden spoon. Do not allow the mixture to boil, or it will curdle.

Remove from the heat, dip the pan into cold water to stop the cooking process, then cool, stir in the cream, add any flavorings, churn, and freeze.

Makes about 4 cups

gelato di strega

Strega is the Italian word for "witch"—and for the flower-flavored liqueur usually served after dinner. Always take care adding alcohol to ices—it lowers the freezing point, so if you add too much to your mixture, it won't freeze properly. If you don't have any Italian Strega available, you could substitute the orange-flavored Grand Marnier. In Italy, they might also substitute liqueurs such as Amaretto or Crème di Cacao.

liqueur-

2 cups *Gelato di crèma* (page 8)
or Rich traditional gelato (page 13)
4 tablespoons Strega or
Grand Marnier

Make the gelato according to the chosen recipe. Stir in the Strega or Grand Marnier, then churn and freeze.
Makes about 2 cups

flavored gelato

tiramisu gelato

Tiramisu is probably Italy's most famous dessert, and beloved of those with a sweet tooth, wherever they live. It is the basis of this thoroughly wicked concoction. Sweet Marsala wine is the traditional flavoring, but rum could also be used.

2 cups sponge fingers

sweet Marsala or rum (see method)

3–6 tablespoons strong espresso coffee, chilled

1 cup mascarpone

1 quantity Zabaglione gelato (page 18)

to decorate

whipped cream

shaved semisweet chocolate

Dip the sponge fingers in Marsala or rum, freeze, then dice.

Mix 3 tablespoons strong espresso coffee with the mascarpone, taste, then add more coffee if preferred.

Make the Zabaglione gelato on page 18, then churn. Remove from the ice-cream machine and spread a layer of mixture over the base of a plastic freezer box or loaf pan. Dot with a layer of diced sponge fingers and a layer of espresso mascarpone. Cover with a second layer of Zabaglione gelato. Repeat as necessary, according to the size of your container. Freeze.

Transfer to the refrigerator for 20 minutes before serving, and decorate with whipped cream and shaved semisweet chocolate.

Serves 6–8

Variation:

Teetotal Tiramisu

Dip sponge fingers in espresso coffee, crumble, then add to 2 cups *Gelato di crèma* on page 8. Sprinkle with drinking chocolate, gently stir into whorls, then freeze. Serve in ice-cream cones.

an amazing

zabaglione gelato

Zabaglione comes from the old Neapolitan dialect and means "great foam". It can also be made with other flavorings—in France it is made with sweet white wine or champagne, and is known as *sabayon*, while in Spain, it is made with sweet sherry.

Alcohol inhibits freezing, so this gelato is quite soft, and may not need to be softened further in the refrigerator before serving.

½ cup sugar, plus

2 tablespoons

1 cup water

3 egg yolks

1 cup heavy cream, lightly whipped

6 tablespoons sweet Marsala

To make the ice-cream, place the sugar and water in a pan and boil until the sugar has completely dissolved. Remove from the heat. Beat the egg yolks until pale and creamy. Beat 2 tablespoons of the hot syrup into the eggs, then gradually beat the egg mixture back into the syrup—the mixture froths, like zabaglione. Fold in the whipped cream and Marsala, then churn and freeze.

Makes about 3 cups

gelato flavor, **wicked** with Marsala

pineapple rum and coconut gelato

The piña colada of gelato—pineapple, rum, and coconut seem to be the very essence of the Caribbean. Make it as an ice-cream, with cream, or as a gelato by mixing it with one of the basic gelato recipes. Serve at a sunny summer lunch in the garden.

Another wonderful flavoring idea is to place 2 vanilla beans in a small bottle of rum and set aside for 1 to 2 days before using. The taste is just like rum and raisin ice-cream!

flesh of ½ small, very ripe pineapple

3 tablespoons freshly grated coconut, or co

shaved coconu

4-6 tablespoo

6 tablespoons

2 drops vanil

2 cups heavy

Italian gelat

Purée the pin
half the sugar. Stir in the ru
using. Taste, and add extra suga ded. Fold into the cream or Traditional Italian gelato, then churn and freeze.

Soften in the refrigerator for 20 minutes, then serve, topped with shaved coconut.

Makes about 4 cups

fruit and

Make these popsicles with any of the flavors in this book, or with peach gelato, as below.

1 lb. ripe peaches
½ cup sugar
water, to cover
2 cups *Gelato di crèma* (recipe page 8)

Place the peaches and sugar in a saucepan with water to cover. Bring to a boil, then simmer until the fruit is cooked but not too soft. Remove from the pan and slip off the skins. Cut in half and remove the pits. Boil the liquid until reduced to about 1 cup, then cool. Purée the fruit in a food processor, adding enough liquid to make 2 cups. Chill.
Make the gelato according to the recipe on page 8, add the peach purée, then churn.
Press the gelato into plastic popsicle molds, cover, and store in the freezer.
Unmold just before serving.
If molds are not available, use small plastic cups and wooden ice-cream sticks.
Makes about 4 cups

fruit popsicles

spice gelato

peaches in sauternes gelato

What do you drink with ices? Remembering that your tastebuds become rather frozen into inaction, it should be strongly flavored and sweet, such as the sauternes used in this recipe, or perhaps a Bellini made with peach liqueur and champagne.

Make this recipe as either a gelato or an ice-cream, according to taste.

1 half bottle sweet dessert wine, such as sauternes

¾ cup sugar

6 yellow peaches

1 cup Rich traditional gelato (page 13), or 1 cup heavy cream

to serve (optional)

sprigs of mint

1 ripe peach, sliced into wedges

Place the wine in a saucepan, add the sugar, heat gently, and stir until dissolved. Add the peaches in a single layer and poach them until cooked but not soft. (Turn them over when half cooked if the liquid does not cover them completely.)

Cool and chill, then slip off the skins, cut in half, and remove the pits. Place the flesh in a blender and purée with enough poaching liquid to make 3 cups. Add sugar to taste.

Mix the purée into either the gelato mixture, or the heavy cream, according to taste.

Churn and freeze. Serve, decorated with the sprigs of mint and peach slices, if using.

Makes about 4 cups

Variation:

Peach Gelato with Peach Eau de Vie

Poach the peaches as above, substituting water for the sweet wine, and adding an extra 2 tablespoons of sugar. Add about 4 tablespoons peach liqueur while churning.

passionfruit grand marnier gelato

Passionfruit and Galliano, the yellow Italian liqueur, is a marriage made in heaven. Don't buy a full-size bottle—just a miniature if you can find one, otherwise a half will last you through many summers. Use Grand Marnier instead if you can't easily find Galliano.

A simple, delicious end to a summer lunch is a large bowl of chilled passionfruit in the middle of the table, a small plate for each person, with an egg cup and a teaspoon. Put a passionfruit in each egg cup, slice off the tops, drip a few drops of Galliano or Grand Marnier into the fruit and eat like a soft-boiled egg. Bliss!

Serve with Galliano Kir—glasses of chilled champagne with a few drops of Galliano.

2 cups *Gelato di crèma* (page 8) or Rich Italian gelato (page 13)

3 oz. passionfruit pulp, with seeds

4 tablespoons Galliano or Grand Marnier, plus extra, to serve

4–6 ripe passionfruit, to serve

Make the chosen gelato and, just before churning, stir in the passionfruit pulp and Galliano or Grand Marnier. Freeze.

Soften in the refrigerator for 10 to 20 minutes before serving with fresh passionfruit, as described left.

Serves 4–6

mascarpone is a wonderful addition to any gelato recipe

mascarpone cognac and clove gelato

This recipe is just divine—so wonderful that I would recommend adding mascarpone to any gelato in this book! I have used rather a large quantity of cloves, because the flavor has to survive both removal of the cloves and freezing—and also because I love the taste of cloves. Use fewer if you wish.

2 cups heavy cream

18 cloves

3 egg yolks

½ cup sugar

1½ cups mascarpone, beaten

1-2 tablespoons cognac (optional)

Heat the cream with the cloves, set aside to infuse for 30 minutes, then strain.

Whisk the egg yolks and sugar together until pale and creamy. Beat in the cream, then cook in a double boiler, stirring constantly, until the mixture coats the back of a wooden spoon. Do not boil or the mixture will curdle. Cool, chill, mix with the mascarpone and cognac, if using, then churn.

Serve immediately or transfer to the freezer. If frozen, soften in the refrigerator for about 20 minutes before serving.

Makes about 4 cups

gingered poache

A variation on the traditional French recipe of pears poached in red wine. Serve the pears with either ginger gelato or the alternative ginger ice-cream.

4–5 pieces stem ginger in syrup
2–3 tablespoons syrup, plus
4 teaspoons, to serve (optional)
2 cups *Gelato di crèma* (page 8)
or ice-cream made from:
2 egg whites (optional—see page 4)
4 tablespoons sugar
1¼ cups heavy cream

gingered poached pears

4 pears
1¼ cups Stones ginger wine
or 1¼ cups water plus 3-inch piece of fresh ginger, sliced
6 tablespoons sugar
1 lemon, sliced
1 cinnamon stick

Purée the ginger and syrup in a blender or food processor. If using *Gelato di crèma*, mix the purée into the gelato, churn, and freeze. If making ice-cream, beat the egg whites until they form soft peaks, then beat in the sugar. In another bowl, whip the cream to a dropping consistency, then fold in the egg white mixture. Churn, then fold in the puréed ginger and the ginger syrup. Taste and add more syrup if preferred. Freeze.

Transfer to the refrigerator for 30 minutes before serving.

To cook the pears, place the ginger wine (or water and fresh ginger) in a pan with the sugar, lemon, and cinnamon stick. Bring to a boil, stirring, until the sugar dissolves. Peel, halve, and core the pears, brushing with lemon juice to prevent browning.

Add the pears to the pan, cover, and simmer for 5 to 10 minutes, or until the fruit is cooked but still firm. Remove with a slotted spoon, cool, and chill.

Serve the pears with a scoop of ginger ice-cream or gelato and a drizzle of ginger syrup.

Serves 4

pears with ginger gelato

almond amaretto gelato

This is one of the most traditional of all Italian gelato flavors. You will find it in *gelateria* shops across Italy—but this one comes courtesy of Nowelle Valentina-Capezza and her children, whose enthusiastic gelato road-tasting has been much appreciated.

1 cup crushed blanched almonds

1 tablespoon Amaretto liqueur

2 cups *Gelato di crèma* (page 8), Traditional Italian gelato (page 10), or Rich traditional gelato (page 13)

Make the chosen gelato and churn. While the paddles are turning, add the Amaretto, and almonds. Continue churning, then freeze. Place in the refrigerator for about 20 minutes before serving.

Makes about 3 cups

chocolate

coffee and nuts

white chocolate and nut gelato

The macadamia nut is native to tropical Australia, and is now grown commercially both there and in Hawaii. Use blanched almonds instead, if preferred. Make sure you use unsalted nuts for this recipe!

2 cups *Gelato di crèma* (page 8)
3 oz. shaved white chocolate, plus extra for serving (optional)
3 oz. sliced macadamia nuts, plus extra for serving (optional)

Make the gelato according to the recipe on page 8. Fold in the chocolate and nuts, then churn and freeze.

Place in the refrigerator for 20 to 30 minutes before serving, and decorate with extra chopped Macadamia nuts and a few shavings of white chocolate, if using.

Makes about 2½ cups

chocolate, ginger, and nougat make

great **gelato** textures

ginger chocolate gelato

Ginger and chocolate make one of the world's great food combinations—another of those marriages made in heaven. If you can't find good ginger chocolates, use stem ginger in syrup and add extra chocolate!

4 oz. ginger chocolates
4 oz. semisweet chocolate, shredded
2 cups *Gelato di crèma* (page 8)
to serve
chocolate curls
sliced stem ginger

Chop the ginger chocolates into generously sized pieces and fold them and the shredded chocolate through the gelato, then churn. Freeze until ready to serve. Soften in the refrigerator for 20 minutes before serving, topped with chocolate curls and ginger.
Makes about 3½ cups

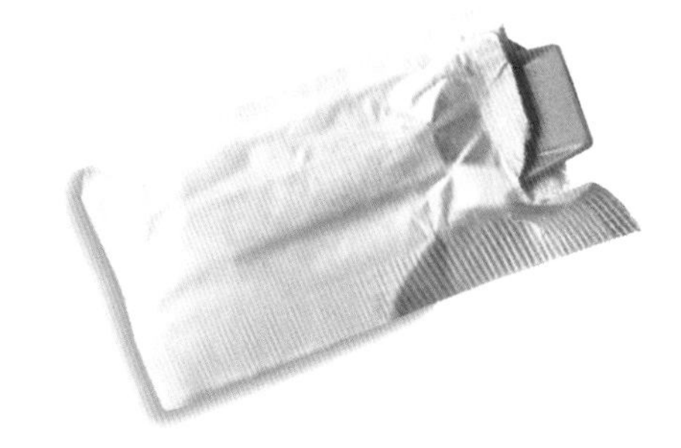

gelato torrone

Torrone is the Italian version of nougat—used in this very traditional gelato recipe.

2 cups Rich traditional gelato (see page 13)
4 oz. torrone or nougat
crushed torrone, to serve

Place the torrone in a paper or plastic bag, and crush with a rolling pin. Stir through the gelato while churning, then freeze. To serve, soften for about 20 minutes in the refrigerator, then serve in scoops, sprinkled with more crushed torrone.
Makes about 2½ cups

chocolate pecan or macadamia brittle ice

An amazing recipe from Zambia in Central Africa, on loan from Stella Shamwana, a great ice-cream creator.

4 egg yolks
4 tablespoons sugar
2 cups heavy cream
3 oz. semisweet chocolate, chopped
nut brittle
peanut oil
6 tablespoons sugar
6 tablespoons water
2 oz. pecan or macadamia nuts, roughly crushed

To make the brittle, place baking parchment on a baking tray and brush with peanut oil. Place the sugar and water in a saucepan, stir well, and bring to a boil over a medium heat. Continue to boil until light brown, then add the crushed nuts. Pour onto the baking tray, let cool, and set, then crush and set aside.
Make the gelato mixture according to the method for *Gelato di crèma* on page 8.
Melt the chocolate in a heatproof bowl set over a saucepan of simmering water.
Cool, add to the basic mixture, add the nut brittle, churn, and freeze.
Soften in the refrigerator for 15 minutes before serving.
Makes about 4 cups

neapolitan espresso gelato

The Neapolitans make some of the world's greatest coffee—strong and black, a little like the inky coffees of Greece and Turkey. Any strong, good coffee suits this recipe.

1 cup heavy cream

3 egg yolks

1 cup sugar, plus extra to taste

1 cup very strong, fresh, espresso coffee, chilled

Heat the cream in a pan to just below boiling point. Beat the egg yolks until creamy, then beat in 1 to 2 tablespoons of the hot cream. Beat in half the remaining cream, then return the egg mixture to the saucepan, beating all the time. Stir in the sugar, then cook in a double boiler, stirring constantly, until the mixture coats the back of a spoon. Remove from the heat, cool, and chill.

Add the coffee, taste, and add extra sugar if required. Churn and freeze.

Makes about 4 cups

capuccino gelato

Capuccino is one of the world's favorite coffees. This ice-cream version is a variation on its theme. Use *Gelato di crèma* or Rich traditional gelato (page 13), as preferred.

2 cups *Gelato di crèma* (page 8)

2 cups Espresso gelato (see left)

to decorate

6 tablespoons whipped cream

shredded chocolate

Serve in one of two ways. Either place scoops of *Gelato di crèma* and Neapolitan espresso gelato in glass coffee cups, the top with whipped cream, and sprinkle with shredded chocolate.

Alternatively, work with slightly softened gelato. Place a layer of Espresso gelato in a *café-au-lait*-style coffee cup.

Top with a second layer of *Gelato di crèma*. Add a spoonful of softly whipped cream and sprinkle with the chocolate.

Makes 4 cups

sorbetto melone

Melons are tricky things to use in ice-creams because their flavor can be very elusive. Choose a very highly flavored variety, such as the orange-fleshed cantaloupe, or one of the sweet, green-fleshed varieties, such as honeydew. Just make sure it is very, very ripe, highly scented, and well chilled.

1 chilled, ripe, scented melon
juice of 1 lemon
4 tablespoons confectioners sugar
1 egg white (optional)

Cut the melon in half and scrape the seeds into a strainer set over a bowl. Pour any juice into the food processor, but discard the seeds. Scoop the melon flesh into the food processor with the confectioners sugar and the lemon juice. Purée, then chill until very cold. Beat the egg white, if using, until until it forms soft peaks, then fold into the melon purée. Churn, and freeze.

Makes about 4 cups

sorbets and sorbetti

italian lemon sorbetto

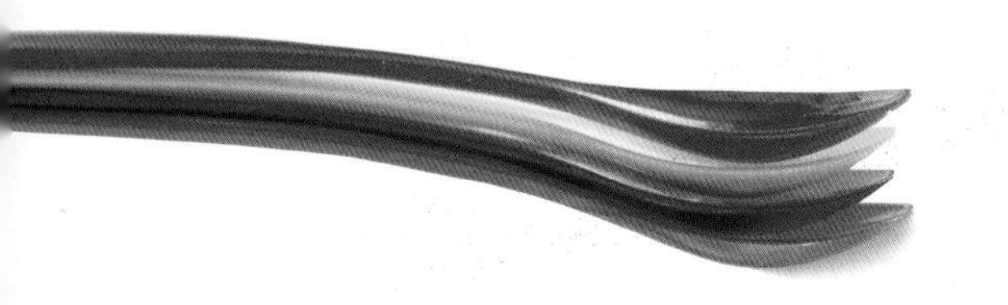

The world's most wonderful recipe for lemon sorbet—courtesy of my Neapolitan cousin!
It is very sweet—so if you prefer yours with a tarter taste, reduce the quantity of sugar, or add a beaten egg white. Filter the mixture before churning if you like, but many people like the extra zip of the lemon zest. When peeling the zest, for this or any other sorbet recipe, make sure no white pith is included—or the sorbetto will be unpleasantly bitter.
A traditional way of serving this recipe is in lemon shells. These are made by slicing a "lid" off the top of each lemon and removing the insides. Freeze the shells first, then pack them with the mixture and freeze. Serve folded in white napkins on small plates.

½ cup water

about 1 cup sugar, or to taste

grated zest of 2 lemons

2 cups freshly squeezed lemon juice

to serve

lemon shells (optional)

Boil the water, sugar, and lemon zest in a pan, stirring until the sugar has dissolved. Cool, chill, then add the lemon juice. Strain if preferred, then churn and freeze.
Soften in the refrigerator for 15 minutes before serving.
Makes about 3½ cups

Variation:
Lime Sorbetto
Substitute a similar quantity of lime juice and zest, and proceed as in the main recipe.

mandarin sorbetto

Always taste the sorbet mixture before freezing, then add more sugar if necessary—remembering it should taste a little sweeter than you would like the end result to be. These three sorbets are my favorites—especially the one made with ruby grapefruit—slightly bitter, and gorgeous with Campari. Serve a selection of flavors for a sunny Italian-style lunch. Italians of course would eat this any time of day, including during the *passegiata*, when everyone takes an evening stroll through the town to show off their new clothes, new babies, new suitors—and to catch up on all the latest gossip.

2 cups freshly squeezed mandarin or tangerine juice plus 1 cup water, or 3 cups mandarin juice
grated zest of 2 mandarins
1 cup sugar, or to taste
1-2 egg whites, beaten (optional)

Place the water, sugar, and mandarin zest in a pan, bring to a boil, and stir well until the sugar has dissolved. Cool, chill, then add the mandarin juice. Strain if liked, add the egg whites if using, then churn and freeze. Soften in the refrigerator for 15 minutes before serving either alone or with other sorbetti.

Makes about 4 cups

Variations:

Red Orange Sorbetto
Substitute 2 cups of orange juice, preferably from red blood oranges, instead of mandarin juice, and proceed as in the main recipe.

Ruby Grapefruit Campari Sorbetto
Substitute 3 cups of ruby grapefruit juice for the mandarin juice and water, and add 1 cup extra sugar. Add 4 tablespoons Campari (optional) after the egg whites, and proceed as in the main recipe.

serve a selection of citrus-flavored sorbetti for a **sunny**

Italian-style lunch

Clockwise from left: Italian lemon sorbetto (page 44), Mandarin sorbetto, Orange sorbetto, and Ruby grapefruit Campari sorbetto (all page 45)

blackberry

and raspberry sorbet

Scandinavia is "berry heaven"—yellow cloudberries are used for jam, and *jordbær* (strawberry) ice-cream and sorbet is made from little, dark red local berries, dripping with ripeness. In Denmark, the sweetened purée from berry fruits is used as a sauce for desserts—I love it with Danish Christmas rice pudding and a sinful concoction of rum, almonds, and cream called *rom fromage*.

In Italy, they make a similar sorbet from a purée of any juicy fruit—try other berries, such as mulberries, or a combination, such as the traditional summer pudding mixture of blackberries, black currants, red currants, strawberries, and raspberries.

In Italy, typical choices would be nectarines (purée with the skin, which makes pretty flecks of red), white peaches, or very ripe apricots. However, I find most apricots taste of cotton wool, and prefer dried soft apricots instead, soaked and poached in water with a little sugar until soft, then puréed.

4 cups blackberries

2 cups raspberries

grated zest and juice of 1 lemon

1½ cups sugar, or to taste

water (see method)

2 tablespoons Framboise (optional)

1-2 egg whites, beaten (optional)

Place the first 4 ingredients in a saucepan, bring slowly to a boil, and simmer for about 2 minutes. Remove from the heat.

Strain into a measuring jug, pressing as much fruit as possible through the strainer. If necessary, add water to achieve 4 cups of pulp. Cool, and stir in the Framboise if using. Taste and add extra sugar if preferred, then chill. Fold the beaten egg whites, if using, into the berry mixture.

Churn and serve immediately, or freeze.

Makes about 4 cups

apple **brandy** sorbet

One of my favourite ices! This is really an English sorbet—made here from Coxes, the finest English apple. Use freshly extracted apple juice (any variety), or a good-quality, freshly squeezed, store-bought juice.

The quantity of sugar will vary, because the apples will vary in sweetness. Taste after 4 tablespoons, and add extra if you think it needs it (remembering that cold dulls the taste). Calvados is apple brandy—but you can use ordinary brandy instead.

4 cups fresh apple juice
4 tablespoons sugar, or to taste
grated rind and juice of 1 lemon
2 very red apples
3 tablespoons Calvados or brandy

Chill all the ingredients. Mix the apple juice with the sugar and brandy until the sugar dissolves. Core the apples, but leave them unpeeled. Either shred them, or purée in the food processor. There should be little flecks of red peel in the purée. Quickly stir in the lemon juice and zest to prevent browning.

Add to the apple juice mixture. Churn and serve immediately, or freeze.

If frozen, soften for a few minutes in the refrigerator before serving.

Makes about 5 cups

Plain yogurt gives one of the more health-conscious versions of ice-cream, with a lovely lemony edge to the taste. If you're worried about eating raw egg white, omit them in this recipe. Though the texture will be different, it will still taste heavenly.

yogurt pineapple ice with mint

1 small, very ripe pineapple
1 cup plain yogurt
1½–2 cups sugar, or to taste
2 egg whites (optional)
2 tablespoons chopped fresh mint leaves

Peel and core the pineapple, and remove the prickly eyes. Whizz in a food processor with 1½ cups of the sugar until smooth and frothy. Remove to a bowl and stir in the yogurt. Taste and add more sugar if necessary.

Beat the egg whites, if using, until frothy and fold into the mixture, together with the chopped fresh mint. Churn and freeze.

Makes about 5–6 cups

asian flavors

orange and cardamom gelato

I'm afraid I've really gone over the top with the cardamom in this gelato—but don't worry, the final effect is fabulous. Cardamom helps to enhance the orange flavor. Always use green cardamom pods. The larger black cardamom pods are also good, but have a slightly coarser flavor.

Wash the oranges well in hot, soapy water to remove any waxy coating before proceeding with the recipe. Remove the zest lightly with a lemon zester, taking care not to include any of the bitter white pith.

To extract the maximum amount of flavor from the cardamom and orange zest, don't strain the mixture until just before churning.

2-3 tablespoons green cardamom pods

zest and juice of 3 oranges

1 cup milk

1 cup heavy cream

3-4 egg yolks

½ cup sugar, or to taste

Place the cardamom pods in a mortar and pestle, mash until all the pods have opened, then remove the green pods and mash the black seeds further.

Place the orange zest and juice in a small saucepan and simmer gently until reduced to about ½ cup. Cool, then chill.

Place the cardamom seeds, milk, and cream in a pan, heat, then set aside to cool and infuse for at least 30 minutes.

Beat the egg yolks until creamy. Reheat the cream, beat 2 tablespoons of cream into the egg mixture, then beat in the remaining cream, little by little.

Stir in the sugar, transfer to a double boiler, and cook, stirring until the mixture coats the back of a spoon. Do not allow to boil, or the mixture will curdle.

Remove from the heat, dip the pan into cold water to stop the cooking process, then cool and chill. When all is well chilled, stir the orange mixture and the custard together, strain, then churn and freeze.

Makes about 4 cups

serve with other **exotic flavors** from Southeast Asia

lemongrass gelato

Lemongrass is one of the herbs typically used in Thai and Vietnamese cooking, and is sold in bigger supermarkets and gourmet shops. Though it does taste of lemon, there is really no substitute for its elusive flavor.

6 stalks of lemongrass
2 cups milk
3-4 egg yolks
¾ cup sugar
1 cup heavy cream

Cut the lemongrass in half lengthwise and bruise it with a rolling pin. Place in a pan with the milk and heat to just below boiling point. Set aside to infuse for 15 minutes. Reheat. Beat the egg yolks and sugar until creamy. Beat 2 tablespoons of the hot milk into the egg mixture, then gradually beat in the remaining milk. Transfer to a double boiler, and cook over a gentle heat, stirring, until the mixture coats the back of a spoon. Taste, adding extra sugar if preferred. Remove from the heat, dip the pan into cold water to stop the cooking process, then cool. Remove the lemongrass - by straining if necessary - then fold the cream into the mixture, churn, and freeze.

Makes about 4 cups

mango ice-cream

Indians are connoisseurs of mangoes—and grow hundreds of different varieties. Some kinds are best used green, for cooking or making chutneys and pickles. Others, rather inelegantly known as "sucking mangoes", are kneaded between the fingers, pierced at one end and the sweet juice sucked out.

The greatest mango of all, however, is the legendary Alphonso, which probably got its name in the former Portuguese colony of Goa, on the west coast of India. Alphonsos are sold in puréed, canned form in Asian supermarkets all over the world, and the flavor is so remarkable you simply can't improve upon it.

If you can't find "Senhor Alphonso", by all means try this recipe with a similar quantity of puréed fresh mango.

This recipe is delicious made with cream or yogurt, and with papaya instead of mango.

4 egg whites (optional)

4 tablespoons sugar

1 cup canned Alphonso mango purée, or fresh mango, puréed

1 cup heavy cream

Beat the egg whites, if using, until frothy. Gradually beat in the sugar. Mix the mango purée with the cream, then fold in the egg white, if using. Churn and freeze.

Makes about 3 cups

Variations:

Mango Yogurt Ice

Use plain yogurt instead of cream. Add extra sugar if necessary, then freeze.

Papaya Ice

Omit the egg whites and, instead of the mango, substitute 1 lb. peeled and seeded papaya. Purée the flesh with the juice of 1 lemon or lime and 1 cup sugar. Mix with the cream, churn, and freeze.

a simple fruit ice makes

a great **tropical** cooler

thai coconut and mango ice

1 cup canned coconut milk

1 cup canned mango purée, or mashed fresh ripe mango flesh

1 cup heavy cream

6 tablespoons desiccated coconut (optional)

Chill all ingredients until very cold. Pour the coconut milk into a bowl and beat. Whip the cream to a dropping consistency. Stir the mango purée into the coconut milk, fold in the cream, and desiccated coconut, if using, then churn.

Makes 3–4 cups

Variation:

Custard Apple Ice

Cut 1 large or 2 small custard apples in half, scoop the flesh into a food processor, but discard the skins and seeds. Whizz the flesh with coconut milk, churn and freeze.

Canned Alphonso mango purée from the recipe on page 58 can be decanted into a plastic container and frozen for future use, or used in this very quick and easy Southeast Asian ice. If you'd prefer not to use coconut milk, use extra cream instead.

The flesh of the custard apple—also known as cherimoya—can be simply puréed with coconut milk and frozen into a spectacular tropical sorbet. Taste before freezing and add a little confectioners sugar if not sweet enough (probably unnecessary, because custard apple is very sweet).

almond and pistachio kulfi

India is one of the great ice-cream nations of the world. Not surprising really, since the cow is a sacred animal there. Their other choice in the milk department is buffalo milk (just like in Italy), and buffalo milk is even richer and healthier than cow's milk.

Indian ice-cream—kulfi—is made of reduced milk, which produces a distinctive cooked-milk flavor.

You can do this yourself (though it's very time-consuming), or use evaporated milk, available in canned or dried form. Or you can enrich ordinary milk with extra powdered milk. I give two methods here, including the traditional one, just in case you have a spare four hours! Use rosewater if you can find it—or vanilla. If you can find kulfi molds, do use them—but any little cups will do instead.

To serve, roll the kulfi molds between your palms, up-end onto small plates and serve immediately (they melt quickly).

1 cup mango purée or 1 tablespoon ground cardamom may be used instead of the other flavoring ingredients.

For the cooked milk:

(1) 12 cups whole milk, plus

~~1 tablespoon arrowroot, or~~

(2) 4 cups whole milk, plus

~~3 oz. powdered milk~~

¾ cup caster sugar

½ oz. shelled, unsalted pistachio nuts, blanched, skinned and crushed

½ oz. blanched almonds, chopped

rosewater or vanilla extract, to taste

For the traditional method (1), pour the milk into a wide, shallow pan, heat to just below boiling point and simmer for 2 to 4 hours until reduced to 4 cups. Mix the arrowroot in a little cold water then stir into the milk. Cook until the mixture thickens like custard.

For method (2), simmer the whole milk until reduced to about 3 cups. Mix the powdered milk with 2 tablespoons hot water until smooth, then stir into the hot milk.

Stir in the sugar until dissolved, then cool and chill the mixture. Stir in the remaining ingredients, pour into molds and freeze.

Serves 6–8

AMAZING!

*Roasted Pistachio's and GROUND up some to a past and put in with milk + egg yolks. No Almonds Combined with Emerald's Recipe

Index

conversion charts

Weights and measures have been rounded up or down slightly to make measuring easier.

VOLUME EQUIVALENTS:

American	Metric	Imperial
1 teaspoon	5 ml	
1 tablespoon	15 ml	
¼ cup	60 ml	2 fl.oz.
⅓ cup	75 ml	2½ fl.oz.
½ cup	125 ml	4 fl.oz.
⅔ cup	150 ml	5 fl.oz. (¼ pint)
¾ cup	175 ml	6 fl.oz.
1 cup	250 ml	8 fl.oz.

WEIGHT EQUIVALENTS:

Imperial	Metric
1 oz.	25 g
2 oz.	50 g
3 oz.	75 g
4 oz.	125 g
5 oz.	150 g
6 oz.	175 g
7 oz.	200 g
8 oz. (½ lb.)	250 g
9 oz.	275 g
10 oz.	300 g
11 oz.	325 g
12 oz.	375 g
13 oz.	400 g
14 oz.	425 g
15 oz.	475 g
16 oz. (1 lb.)	500 g
2 1b.	1 kg

MEASUREMENTS:

Inches	Cm
¼ inch	5 mm
½ inch	1 cm
¾ inch	1.5 cm
1 inch	2.5 cm
2 inches	5 cm
3 inches	7 cm
4 inches	10 cm
5 inches	12 cm
6 inches	15 cm
7 inches	18 cm
8 inches	20 cm
9 inches	23 cm
10 inches	25 cm
11 inches	28 cm
12 inches	30 cm

OVEN TEMPERATURES:

225°F	110°C	Gas ¼
250°F	120°C	Gas ½
275°F	140°C	Gas 1
300°F	150°C	Gas 2
325°F	160°C	Gas 3
350°F	180°C	Gas 4
375°F	190°C	Gas 5
400°F	200°C	Gas 6
425°F	220°C	Gas 7
450°F	230°C	Gas 8
475°F	240°C	Gas 9